L
I
F
E
V
I
E
W
S

Published by Creative Education
123 South Broad Street, Mankato, Minnesota 56001
Creative Education is an imprint of The Creative Company

Art direction by Rita Marshall; Production design by The Design Lab

Photographs by Jay Ireland & Georgienne Bradley, Eugene G. Schulz,
Tom Stack & Associates (Erwin & Peggy Bauer, Chip & Jill Eisenhart, Jeff Foott,
Kitchin & Hurst, Joe McDonald, Greg Vaughn, Dave Watts)

Library of Congress Cataloging-in-Publication Data

George, Michael.
Rainforests / by Michael George.
p. cm. — (LifeViews)
Summary: Describes the plant and animal life, as well as the climate, of rain forests. Includes related activities.
Includes bibliographical references (p.).
ISBN 1-58341-252-2
1. Rain forests—Juvenile literature. [1. Rain forests.] I. Title. II. Series.
QH86 .G46   2003
577.34—dc21   2002034790

First Edition

2 4 6 8 9 7 5 3 1

MANY PEOPLE IMAGINE

tropical rainforests as the settings for **adventure** movies, filled with strange plants, deadly animals, and savage ape-men. Yet despite their attempts, moviemakers cannot accurately portray the **excitement** of an actual tropical rainforest. It is more amazing than anything that can be shown on a screen.

Upon entering a tropical rainforest, people smell the aroma of flowers and hear the singing of birds. At first, the forest appears damp, dark, and gloomy. But as people's eyes adjust to the dim forest interior, they notice brightly colored flowers amid striking shades of green. Everywhere they look there are

Heat and moisture encourage rainforest growth.

creatures creeping, crawling, jumping, and flying. **Monkeys** swing through the trees, ants parade across the ground, and butterflies flutter through the air. The tropical rainforest is filled with an extravaganza of wonderful life.

Tropical rainforests are appropriately named—they are all located in Earth's tropical regions, between the Tropic of Cancer and the Tropic of Capricorn. They cover large areas of Central and South America, Asia, Africa, and many islands in the Pacific Ocean. The **Amazon** is the largest tropical rainforest in the world. It covers a region in South America that is nearly as large as the continental United States.

Located near the **equator**, tropical rainforests do not have seasons as most people know them. The temperature stays near 80 °F (27 °C), summer and winter, and plants are green all year long. Rather than being defined by average temperatures, seasons in the tropics are determined by the amount of rainfall. Over an entire year, most tropical forests receive more

More than 50 percent of Earth's species live in rainforests. Unfortunately, at the rate humans are destroying tropical forests, animals such as the toucan (top) and red-eyed tree frog (bottom) could one day become extinct.

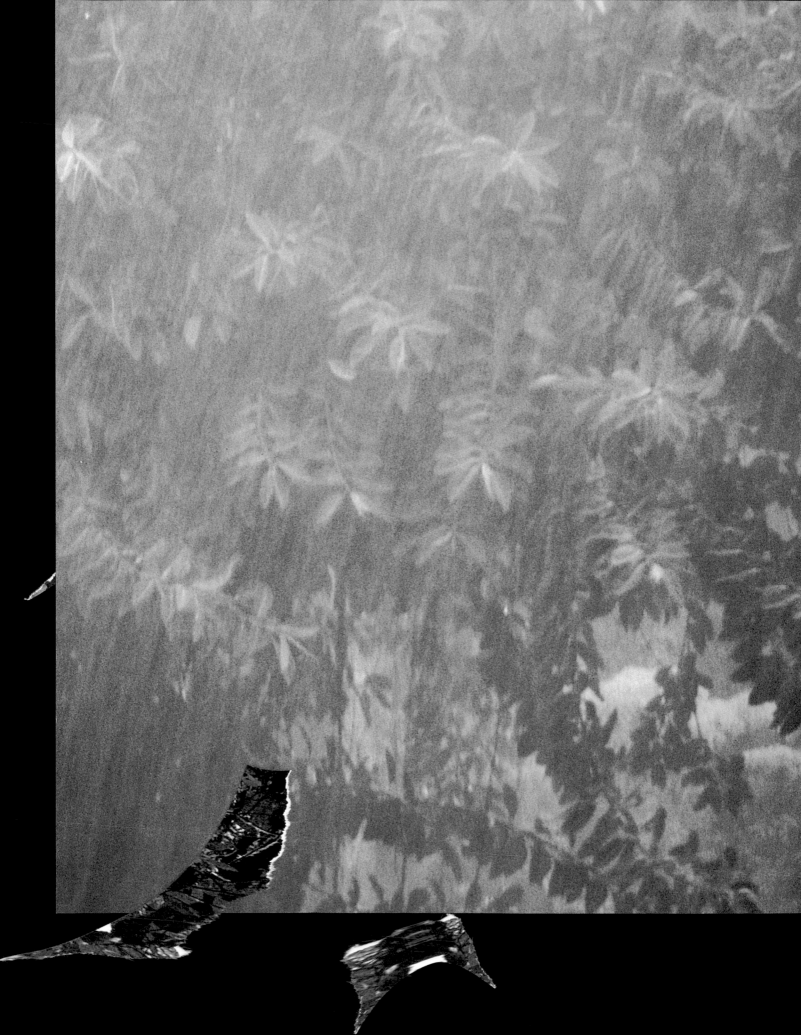

than 80 inches (200 cm) of precipitation. Most of this moisture falls during the rainy season, when water may pour from the sky for days on end. Although there is less precipitation during the dry season, there are still drenching rains every few days.

Blessed with warm temperatures and abundant rainfall, the tropical forest has a **climate** that is ideal for life. As a result, an astonishing variety of organisms inhabit tropical forests. In fact, of all the known **species** of plants and animals in the world, about half live in tropical rainforests. From beneath the forest floor to the tops of the tallest trees, tropical forests teem with life.

In order to classify and study this abundance of life, scientists divide tropical forests into four main levels: ground, low forest, mid-forest, and canopy. Each level of the forest has its own characteristic **vegetation** and animal life.

Ground level is the lowest layer of the tropical rainforest. Many people assume that the only way to travel through a rainforest is by swinging a machete, hacking through thick

About an inch and a half (3.8 cm) of rain falls in a rainforest each week. Because of the canopy's dense vegetation, it may take the rain as long as 10 minutes to reach the ground.

vines and vegetation. This image, however, is not typical of tropical rainforests. In most areas, a thick covering of leaves, suspended high in the air, prevents sunlight from reaching the ground. Since plants cannot grow without sunlight, most of the forest floor has little vegetation. The ground is covered by only a thin layer of dead leaves.

Although the forest floor is generally bare, thick undergrowth does occur along the edges of the forest, on river banks, and in isolated clearings. In these areas, sunlight

slices through the thick covering of forest leaves, and an upsurge of plants struggles for **survival**.

Whether it is bare or entangled with vegetation, the forest floor is inhabited by many interesting and important creatures. Most of the organisms that live on the ground are **decomposers**, tiny creatures that feed on dead plant and animal material. They include a variety of

Plants are the foundation upon which the rest of the rainforest is built. Plants are eaten by herbivores, who, in turn, are eaten by carnivores, who eventually die and decompose, enriching the soil for future plant growth.

insects, bacteria, and fungi. These organisms are so abundant that dead leaves and small animals rarely remain on the ground for more than a day.

In addition to these tiny housekeepers, the forest floor is also inhabited by a variety of larger creatures. Elephants, hippopotamuses, and **water buffaloes** live on the floor of the African and Asian rainforests. The ground level of the Amazon forest is home to smaller animals, including armadillos, raccoonlike coatimundis, and a variety of tropical rodents. The most ferocious inhabitant of the Amazon forest floor is the peccary, a wild pig armed with razor-sharp tusks. After nightfall, packs of peccaries roam the forest in search of food.

Located a few feet above the ground is the low-level forest. Here, colonies of insects live among odd-looking bushes and shrubs that are found no place else on Earth. Most plants in the low-level forest have broad, leathery leaves. The wide leaves help the plants absorb what little light there is in the dim forest interior. Unlike the bushes of temperate forests, tropical shrubs are unusually large; many species grow to the

Native to the swampy areas surrounding South American rainforests, the capybara (top) is the world's largest rodent. It lives and feeds on the forest floor, as do the water buffalo (left) and armadillo (right).

size of mature apple trees. Even tropical grasses are oversized; **bamboo**, a type of grass that thrives in East African forests, can grow as tall as a four-story building.

Above the plants of the low-level forest, slender tree trunks stretch toward the sky. Covered with mosses and lichens, the tree trunks provide ideal hiding places for tropical insects. Many of these creatures are so well **camouflaged** that they are nearly invisible. However, the mid-level forest is also patrolled by keen-eyed birds looking for a tasty snack. Many of these tropical birds are decorated with blue, yellow, green, and red feathers. The brilliant colors help the birds blend in with the forest's flowers and leaves. The colors also help the birds attract mates.

Located above the open spaces of the mid-level forest is the canopy, the topmost level of a tropical forest. The canopy itself contains various layers of vegetation. The lowest layer hangs 50 to 60 feet (15–18 m) above the ground. These leaves are usually so thick that a person on the forest floor cannot see through them. The middle layer of the canopy

Once the sacred bird of the ancient Mayas and Aztecs, the brilliantly colored quetzal is now found only in remote rainforests of Central America. Listed as endangered, the quetzal's future is uncertain.

consists of taller trees, species that stretch up to 100 feet (30 m) above the ground. Beyond this thin layer of leaves lies the upper canopy, the highest level of a tropical forest. Here, trees up to 200 feet (61 m) tall tower above the dense lower canopies.

Bathed in warm sunshine, the forest canopy differs greatly from the dark and gloomy forest interior. Besides receiving more sunlight, the top of the forest also receives more moisture than the forest floor. Some of the rain that falls on a tropical forest never reaches the ground because it is absorbed by the leaves and branches of the canopy trees.

The canopy also differs from the forest interior in that it is caressed by warm tropical breezes. In order to withstand the stronger winds that accompany storms, canopy trees have developed unusual methods of support. The tallest trees have wide, winglike extensions at the bases of their trunks. These extensions, called **buttresses**, help support the tall trunks and heavy branches. Other trees have pitchfork-like roots that provide extra stability in wet, swampy soils.

Often towering more than 165 feet (50 m) above the ground, canopy trees grow thick, far-reaching roots to stabilize themselves. Lianas, vines that can exceed eight inches (20 cm) in diameter, also support the giant trees.

Tropical trees are also reinforced by **lianas**, cablelike vines that are tangled in the leaves and branches of the canopy. Some of these vines are as thick as telephone poles, and many are hundreds of feet long. Lianas are so strong that if a tree breaks off at its base, it often remains standing, suspended by the vines.

Trees and lianas are not the only plants that make up the forest canopy. Many smaller plants actually grow on the branches and leaves of the canopy trees. Scientists call these plants epiphytes, or air plants. They include a wide variety of **orchids**, ferns, and bromeliads (tropical plants that are related to the pineapple).

Suspended high above the ground, epiphytes take advantage of the canopy's abundant sunshine and moisture. Rather than burrowing into the ground, an epiphyte's roots wrap around tree trunks and branches. The roots anchor the plant to the canopy and absorb moisture from the **humid** forest air. They also extract nutrients from the debris that collects in the crooks and crannies of tree limbs. Besides nourishing epiphytes, this

Beetles and other insects make up the largest group of animals in the rainforest ecosystem. They live within every level of the forest, from the ground level to the canopy.

treetop soil shelters a variety of animals, including **spiders**, insects, and even earthworms.

Insects and other small animals are not the only creatures that inhabit the forest canopy. In fact, of all the creatures that live in the Amazon rainforest, more than half reside in the canopy. The treetops house an assortment of monkeys, birds, frogs, snakes, and **lizards**. Some of these animals never venture to the ground below. Night and day, the canopy is filled with the sounds of animals.

From the forest floor to the canopy treetops, the tropical rainforest is filled with a fascinating variety of organisms. All of these creatures depend on each other in intricate ways. Trees need lianas for support, many animals require plants for food, and all the organisms depend on decomposers to return important nutrients to the soil. But with so many organisms living in one place, there is also fierce **competition** for food and space. Survival in a tropical forest is a difficult game. Another enemy is lurking behind every leaf.

For survival in the forest, speed and strength are helpful,

No ecosystem in the world has greater diversity among its plants and animals than the rainforest. Large forests such as the Amazon may be home to more than 10 million animal species.

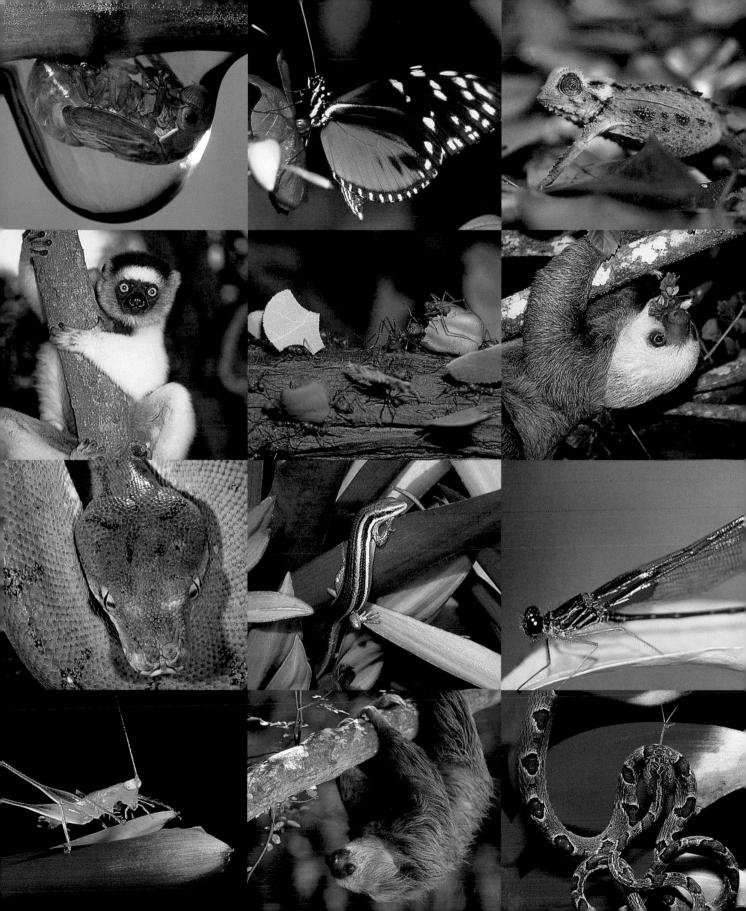

but they are not always enough. Staying alive also requires keen **senses** and effective methods of finding food and avoiding enemies. Some creatures fool their enemies with unusual disguises. Other forest animals are camouflaged. By blending into the surroundings, they increase both their chances of finding food and their chances of avoiding enemies. Rather than trying to hide, many poisonous animals do all they can to be noticed. They display brilliant colors to warn enemies of their unpleasant taste.

Within the tropical rainforest some species are friends, and some are enemies, but all the creatures depend on each other in many ways. Because of this intricate **balance**, tropical rainforests have endured for hundreds of millions of years, longer than any other **habitat** on Earth. Unfortunately, the future of Earth's tropical rainforests is not guaranteed.

In a quest for lumber and farmland, people are destroying Earth's tropical rainforests. Every minute, bulldozers and fires clear another 50 acres (20 ha) of tropical land. The nutrients that are necessary for life are burned or are carried away in

Between 1980 and 1990, large-scale deforestation (removal of trees) destroyed a section of Brazilian rainforest almost equal to the total area of North and South Dakota combined. As a result, thousands of species disappeared forever.

trucks. Any nutrients that remain are washed away by the daily rains. Lacking these important nutrients, the land cannot be reforested, and the soil cannot support crops for more than two or three seasons. Once destroyed, a tropical forest is lost forever, along with countless species of plants and animals. All that remains is barren, lifeless soil.

For hundreds of millions of years, tropical rainforests have supported countless **generations** of plants and animals. During this time many species have become **extinct**, but the forest has always welcomed new inhabitants who have the tools for survival. However, in their long history, the tropical forests have never seen a creature as ruthless as modern man. We alone are responsible for the future of the tropical rainforests, the world's most diverse and remarkable habitat.

Rainforest bamboo can grow nine inches (23 cm) per day.

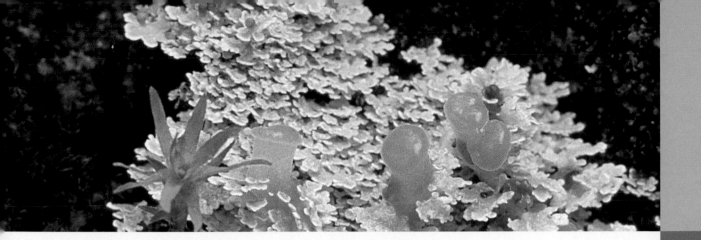

Observation

Plants need water, light, and air to survive, but, as you saw in this experiment, they do not necessarily need soil. In a soil-less environment, plants can obtain the nutrients they need through liquid or granular plant food. Or, high above the forest floor, they can extract nutrients from debris caught in the crooks of tree limbs. Although they don't need soil, plants do need some sort of support. Growing mediums, such as the vermiculite, perlite, or peat moss you used, anchor plant roots so the growing plants don't topple over. They also retain moisture and, because they're less dense than soil, allow for the easy exchange of oxygen and other important gases to and from plant roots. In the rainforest canopy, tree trunks and branches keep epiphytes anchored.

Hydroponics, the science of growing plants without soil, has increased in popularity over the past few years for many reasons: it requires less space than traditional soil methods and can be set up on land ill-suited for plowing; it allows for more control over the nutrients growing plants receive; it can produce healthier, pesticide-free products through use of biological pest control; and it has no dependence on the weather, enabling crop production year-round.

LIGHT MAZE

Plants have a strong urge to grow toward light. Guided by special light-sensitive cells within their leaves and stems, plants twist and turn to maximize their exposure to light, no matter how small the source.

For this activity, find a shoe box and cut a hole about the size of a quarter in the center of one end. Next, cut two cardboard dividers so that they fit snugly in the box. Cut a quarter-sized hole in the far right side of one divider and a hole on the far left side of the other divider. Plant a sprouting potato in a small pot filled with moist soil and place it in a corner of the box opposite the end hole. Close the box and set it in a sunny location, the end hole facing the sun.

Check the box after a few days. Even though the amount of light passing through the box is quite small, its effect on the plant is powerful. In tropical rainforests, most of the forest floor receives no light and is bare, but along the edge of the forest and in isolated clearings where a few sunbeams do break through, plants fight for the light, and plant growth explodes in thick, tangled bunches.

LEARN MORE ABOUT RAINFORESTS

Educational Web Adventures:
    Amazon Interactive
(Internet resource for information on the
    Ecuadorian Amazon)
http://www.eduweb.com/amazon.html

Journey into Amazonia
(Online visit to the world's largest
    tropical rainforest)
http://www.pbs.org/journeytoamazonia

Rainforest Action Network
221 Pine Street, Suite 500
San Francisco, CA 94104
http://www.ran.org

Rainforest Alliance
65 Bleecker Street
New York, NY 10012
http://www.rainforest-alliance.org

Rainforest Conservation Fund
2038 North Clark Street, Suite 233
Chicago, IL 60614
http://www.rainforestconservation.org

The Rainforest Foundation UK
City Cloisters, Suite A5
196 Old Street
London EC1V9FR
United Kingdom
http://www.rainforestfoundationuk.org

INDEX

Amazon, 8, 14, 21
animals, 7–8, 11, 12, 14, 17,
    21–22, 25, 26
    adaptations, 22, 25
    birds, 7, 17, 21
    peccaries, 14
decomposers, 12
hydroponics, 29
insects, 8, 12, 14, 17, 21
levels
    canopy, 11, 17–18, 21, 28
    ground, 11–12, 14
    low forest, 11, 14
    mid-forest, 11, 14, 17
locations, 8
precipitation, 8, 11, 18
rainfall, *see precipitation*

rainforests
    destruction of, 25
    future of, 25–26
relationships, 22, 25
seasons, 8, 11
sizes, 8
storms, 18
temperatures, 8
trees, 14, 17, 18, 21
    buttresses, 18
    lianas, 18
vegetation, 11–12, 14, 17, 18,
    21, 28, 30
    air plants, *see vegetation, epiphytes*
    bamboo, 14
    epiphytes, 21, 28
    and light, 30
    shrubs, 14
vines, *see trees, lianas*

Rainforests are the world's most precious jewels.